Glencoe

The Changing Moods

'*Thousands of tired, nerve-shaken, over-civilised people are beginning to find out that going to the mountains is going home; that wilderness is a necessity; and that mountain parks and reservations are useful not only as fountains of lumber and irrigating rivers, but as fountains of life.*'

JOHN MUIR, 1901.
The Scots-born American now widely recognised as the father of conservation was seeking to protect the wilds of Yosemite Valley and the Sierra Nevada from further commercial exploitation.

COE

The Changing Moods

Alan Thomson

Lochar Publishing
Moffat · Scotland

For my wife Ann and sons
Colin, Malcolm and Graham

Acknowledgements

This I freely confess, is a subjective, selective and highly empathetic view of perhaps Scotland's best-loved and internationally renowned sanctuary. No man is an island and many, through friendship, acquaintance or their own writings have helped author this book. Especially I thank Ed Drummond, John Grieve, John Hardie, Peter Hodgkiss, Hamish MacInnes, Bill Murray and Alex Small.

©Alan Thomson, 1990

Published by Lochar Publishing Ltd MOFFAT DG10 9JU

Designed by Hammond Hammond

British Library Cataloguing in Publication Data
Thomson, Alan, 1939–
Glencoe: the changing moods.
1. Scotland. Highland
Region. Ben Nevis & Glencoe
– Visitor's guides
I. Title
914.1185

ISBN 0-948403-26-8

Typeset in Baskerville by Chapterhouse and printed in Scotland by
Scotprint Ltd, Musselburgh

CONTENTS

CHAPTER ONE

The Changing Moods

Alternative garb of Buachaille Etive Mor. Pale grey-pink in summer, the great Stob Dearg pyramid between Glen Coe and Glen Etive presents a chill white shoulder in winter.

BUACHAILLE ETIVE MOR rises starkly mauve across the frosted heather, a stoic herdsman guarding through a bleak night the exposed approach to lower Glen Coe. Sheets of ice like shattered windscreens tilt gently against the boulders of the River Coupall and give an occasional, muted creak. Some red deer hinds arrive to forage under Great Gully. Eventually, the first dawn rays strike the crest of Crowberry Tower and torch a beacon for the few quietly spaced-out drivers on the A82 this early in the day – or the year, for that. Set in such splendid isolation on the fringe of Rannoch Moor, the elegant pyramid casts a long shadow. It is easily the West Highland's most striking mountain.

Over the years, the Buachaille has become part of my spiritual home. Tall and silent, self-reliant, staunch to the end, he is no mere fair-weather friend. Hurtful to those who fall from grace, he can be a mortal enemy to the incompetent, the careless or those just unlucky enough to stumble on his tracks.

Frequenters of the glen are walkers, climbers and skiers or have some kindred mountain interest; in serious cases an obsession. The bulk of visitors, though, are likely only to know the great herdsman waiting at the nexus of Glen Etive and Glen Coe in his summer garb. Habitues will mostly yield, I fancy, that the Buachaille and his scattered mountain flock are more vivid off-season from late February to April, when the sun creeps back to the hemisphere and the snow sets firm. Then the hills quieten and those fortunate or determined enough to reach the Argyll heights midweek, can appreciate them as nature surely intended. In comparative solitude.

Glencoe itself is a haven for all seasons, and offers an enthralling gamut of moods. Sometimes, most of them on the same day. Now, of course, it is virtually a world resort. It is Scotland's best-known glen internationally and is arguably its best-loved, though a rare visitor is heard to concur with Charles Dickens. On a Highland tour of 1841 he found the glen desolate, its strewn boulders like giant's tombstones.

From above the Meeting of Three Waters, Stob Coire nan Lochan emerges beyond Beinn Fhada (left) and the sunlit cast face of Gearr Aonach. These ridges and cliffs are delights to walkers and climbers in all seasons. The steep Broad Gully (distant left-centre) has been skied.

Overleaf: Below the Gorge, the shadowed north faces of Gearr Aonach and Aonach Dubh (left) gaze across the River Coe to the slopes of Aonach Eagach.

Not every early traveller was subdued. Samuel Coleridge who came sightseeing to romantic Scotland, like the Wordsworths in 1803, was a shade blasé. A keen Lakeland explorer prone even in that era to scramble on Scafell, the poet and critic found the glen not precipitous or craggy enough for his taste. This aberration would have aroused ire among rock and ice tigers of modern times who disport on a veritable tidal wave of steep and challenging cliffs. Most likely, Coleridge's pique at the peaks, unsustained by any similar literary review, stemmed from the vapours.

Today's travellers arrive by every means; foot, bike, car and coach. They cruise from the Clyde and flock by rail across the boggy Moor of Rannoch to Fort William, then south again. Even by air they come. Civilian helicopters along with RAF rescue aircraft land. Jets thunder through, (to regular protest from the rural populace) on training flights. Mountaineers enjoy the frisson of sometimes looking down on combat planes.

A seasonal count of people entering the National Trust for Scotland's tourist centre at Clachaig near the foot of the glen in 1989, was 160,000. An informed guess at the entire year-round influx suggests maybe ten times that figure. Though the area's economy is much boosted by the host of holiday season incomers, there are rumblings of late among those jealous of such a precious Highland fastness that tourism has attained the status of pollution. Some call on the principal custodian, the NTS, to ensure that Glencoe and kindred rare places are no longer commercially promoted like stately homes and museums. But we come to that later.

Such international affection arises in part from the historic outrage against the Macdonalds, conspired at by two powerful Campbells, the Earls of Stair and Breadalbane. The infamy of the massacre of February 13, 1692, and that despicable breach of Highland hospitality inspire universal disdain. As acts of cynicism and political expediency they rank with recent events in Eastern Europe and China.

But the weeping glen's worldly fame rests deservedly on more than the massacre of the MacIan, old Alastair, 12th clan chief of the Macdonalds of Glencoe and 37 or so of his kin around dawn on a foul winter's morn. Or alone on Robert Louis Stevenson's allusions in *Kidnapped* and *Catriona* to the killing of the Red Fox, and the hanging for that enigmatic murder of James Stewart of Aucharn, whose monument stands forlornly above my house at Ballachulish Bridge.

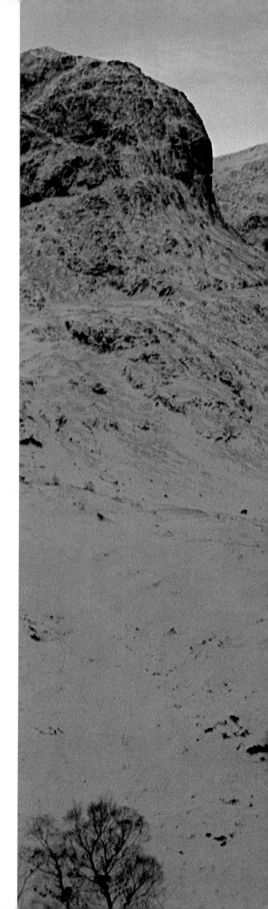

Glencoe is foremost a West Highland Xanadu for walkers, skiers and mountaineers. Fishermen, birdwatchers, botanists, geologists, wildlife enthusiasts and those who simply thrive on majestic landscape, in freeze, mist or scorching sun, all find a sanctum. I marvel at its diverse topography, the hanging valleys, airy aretes, gorges, shady defiles, lochs, jagged ridges, the rolling moors, tarns and tundra. A dedicated incumbent, I am never bored here. What inner Glen Coe may lack, greater Glencoe stretching, in my view, east from Loch Linnhe across Rannoch Moor and south from the Mamores to Glen Kinglass and Loch Tulla, will provide.

In general the glen's hospitality, violation of which was close to treason by 17th Century tradition, remains expansive, even to Campbells. A former owner of the popular Clachaig Inn, the effusive Rory Macdonald, delighted in a reception notice that stated blandly, 'No Hawkers or Campbells'. It is still there to provoke, but only amusement. For those who demur at B&B, varied small guesthouses

Glencoe village in the 17th Century was a handful of intimate clan 'townships' scattered in the glen. Rose Cottage (above) at Upper Carnoch, a stony place, is a traditional restored cottage.

and a clutch of hotels, the area has two excellent camping and caravan sites, near Achnacon and Invercoe on the Kinlochleven road. A bunkhouse and commendable youth hostel sit by the single-track road between the Achnambeithach bridge on the A82 and Glencoe village.

Fly camping is popular with climbers and walkers, notably near the inn, though summer pollution there is becoming intolerable. Police are liable to collar those who leave vehicles obstructing passing places. Enticement to tent on the old, once-designated massacre site at Clachaig is the proximity to a pub. Added inducement is the view from the lounge to Aonach Dubh over a cooling drink, or hot snack depending on the rigour of your day on the hill.

Incurable voyeurs will note that the prospect of Buachaille Etive Mor from the resident's lounge of Scotland's oldest inn, the King's House at the head of the glen, is equally if not more admirable, so accounts are square. Most visitors congregate, however, in the lower glen beneath the dominant heights of Aonach Dubh's west face. This

Maj. Eric Moss (left) leads Glasgow Society Clan Donald at Bridge of Coe to mark the anniversary of the infamous massacre of February 13, 1692. Clachaig Inn (above), an old horse-changing post, is a popular hosteiry today with walkers and climbers.

reflects the ever-changing moods of Glen Coe through the seasons. Towering cliffs rise sheer in spectacular buttresses above reedy, reflective Loch Achtriochtan and the mottled green strath that drains an often turbulent River Coe.

The River Coe, a popular water for salmon fishers, cascades at Clachaig under the Aonach Eagach.

Fresh salmon waters from the glen's copious rains (more than 90 inches a year!) and the snows of remote deer corries splash between narrow, rhyolite and granite banks, fringed with birch, rowan and alder. In spate they cascade over splendid falls, notably at The Gorge and above Achnambeithach, and rush to dilute the salinity of Loch Leven. The blending is at Invercoe below the old Carnoch townships, now commonly known as Glencoe village.

Aonach Dubh, the dark ridge of the Gaelic but only in mourning, happens mostly to be a warm grey-pink and commands superlative views. The buttresses are relics of a primordial cauldron-subsidence and rank with Buachaille Etive Mor, above the watershed, among the most impressive scenery of their kind in Britain. The western cliffs give fine vistas on clear days to the twin, Munro-bagging peaks of the Bheinn a' Bheithir horseshoe, or the thunderbolt hill my often boisterous neighbour above Ballachulish narrows.

Invercoe on Loch Leven (above), the accepted site o the old Macdonald chiefs' principal residence. There is now a well-serviced caravan and camping site here below the Pap of Glencoe and the distant snows of Na Gruagaichean.

A typical summer welcome for tourists at the pipers' lay-by beneath Aonach Dubh and Coire Lochan (right).

The panorama ranges across Loch Linnhe to wild Ardgour and Ardnamurchan, the most westerly edge of the British mainland. This beguiling hinterland over Corran vehicular ferry is refreshingly devoid of the bulk of tourists on the grand Highland tour, though the folk of Acharacle and Kilchoan greatly deplore their negligence. Just south of the estimable volcanic pile of Aonach Dubh lurks the andesite fortress of Bidean nam Bian, the peak of the peaks, secluded high in beckoning corries beyond Stob Coire nan Lochan.

Obscured from the A82 which permits only a glimpse of the citadel from the Clachaig road end, Bidean nam Bian at 3,776 ft is the loftiest summit in Argyll. This distinction, its obvious Munro* status, and the fact that it stands at the apex of the glen's famous Three Sisters ensures the peak a constant stream of summiteers throughout the year.

The massif of Bidean nam
Bian, including Stob Coire nan
Lochan, Aonach Dubh and Stob
Coire nan Beith, rises beyond
walkers on the Sgorr Bhan arete
above Ballachulish.

*Munros – all 277 Scots peaks
rising to 3,000 ft and above

Even on a bright Saturday in February I have counted a general assembly from the peak's satellites of up to 40 people around the cairn embracing the views to Mull, Skye and the distant Hebrides.

At the mountain's left shoulder, the squat cone of Stob Coire nam Beith, the peak of the birch corrie, arcs down to the long promontory of An t-Sron and the obvious granite margin of the great cauldron collapse. The bold, at times menacing character of Glen Coe – especially under storm – here, and for nine miles farther east, up past the Three Sisters through the shadowy defile to the two Buachailles, père et fils, is largely contained within a remarkable, 30-square-mile enclosure of lava.

It was designer-hewn by weather and glacial erosion to attain the magnificence we observe and appreciate today. If a single masterpiece in oils and canvass by Picasso or Van Gogh can be priced at auction above £25 m, what value to the nation this eternal glen? In the 1930s, Percy Unna, an English civil engineer of Danish extraction recognised how rare an artifact Glencoe was in Britain's rich landscape heritage and through the Scottish Mountaineering Club, whose president he became, and the National Trust for Scotland he orchestrated its purchase. His stipulation that the acquisition, ultimately to reach 14,200 acres of comparative wilderness, should remain as wild as possible had wide-reaching implications that arouse controversy even now.

Opposite Aonach Dubh, defending the northern ramparts of Glen Coe is the serrated and airy Aonach Eagach. The exciting three-mile traverse of the notched ridge is immensely popular with walkers of varied experience. In winter it has a pervasive Alpine atmosphere and should be approached with respect.

Just about every Gaelic reference in this text to specific features of the West Highland landscape, be it mountain, lochan or heath is something more a designation, or description, rather than simply a name. There are few Mount Everests or McKinleys in Gaeldom, just as these are excluded or are scarce in the topographical traditions of the

Overleaf: Garbh Bheinn and Coire Dubh across Loch Linnhe in Ardgour are often striking against cloud and the slanting evening light.

The A82 Glasgow-Fort William road passes directly below Aonach Dubh (above) viewed across the River Coe.

Nepalese and the Inuit, or Eskimo. Gaelic oral culture produced Buachaille Etive Mor, an appellation marginally more liquid than The Great Herdsman of Etive.

Poetic and emotive titles are fairly common, though in general Highland descriptions are short and practical suggesting primarily a location by colour, shape, height or some similar natural attribute. Myth and historic significance are equally relevant. Tongue-twisters though some are, notably to those who live furth of Scotland, they are worth taking the time to absorb. While Gaelic is under threat or direct assault on a wide front and defences are raised in Skye, Lewis and Inverness, it is worth saying that nowhere is it more staunchly defended by the Sassenach than in its rich mountain nomenclature.

Mountain architecture, like all things aesthetic, either dilates or abates in the eye of the beholder. Every Glencoe peak has instrinsic quality of its own and a plethora of admirers. Though the Buachaille undoubtedly has the finer profile, I have a predilection for an aspect of Aonach Dubh. Its vistas are much better and no precipice in Glencoe has quite the enfolding ambiance of the dark cliffs, so girded around with drama.

A putative residence of the legendary Gaelic warrior and bard, Ossian's Cave is a gaping facial scar beloved of visitors high on the brow of Aonach Dubh. It was first attained by Carnoch shepherd Nicol Marquis as early as 1868. In the gloaming it gently fades just as the full aura of the west face is manifest in the dipping light. The cave is no climb for novices.

Many will challenge my sentiment and state preference entirely for the sheer symmetry of the Buachaille. And that is their prerogative. I am ready to admit it takes a diamond to cut a diamond.

In spate, the Allt Lairig Eilde tumbles into the River Coe at the Gorge, a camera haunt of tourists, below Beinn Fhada.

Glen Coe (left) looking east from the heights of Sgor nam Fiannaidh to Buachaille Etive Mor and the plain of Rannoch Moor.

CHAPTER TWO

Shadows on the Wall

The Rive Coe curves near Clachaig toward the green strath of Achnacon – the field of dogs. Davy Gunn (above) elegantly ascends 'Line-up' on the Rannoch Wall.

Will Thomson garbed '70s-style for a bleak traverse of Beinn Fhada, the long ridge. Beyond, Ben Nevis sulks.

BIG CLOUDS HANG-GLIDING on an affable breeze cast

spectres of light and shade across Aonach Dubh, the most westerly and spectacular of the Three Sisters, the irascible triplets who dominate the lower glen. Volcanic faces between the gullies of Middle Ledge sulk as the shadows drift, then blush and beam again in the wind-fanned embers of the day. A fire glows brightest just before it dies. From a stance on the colossus, 1,000 ft or so above the road, the straying firmament gently animates these old igneous walls. Magical sculpture carved by ice, water and time seems languidly to rotate as if something cosmic activates the whole austere structure; or is it a figment of a highly impressionable mind?

Moving usually alone but not lonesome in the Bidean massif has become fairly habitual over the years since I came permanently to the glen. Walking and scrambling on the peaks is a highly therapeutic activity despite the exertion, or more aptly because of it, as many who flock there know. But to climb on the statues in reliable company would be my choice by far.

Starting on a route, usually after midday in winter and much later when the days begin to stretch is not exclusively a personal defect. It is endemic to a breed of reasonably experienced Scots. Tyros, I should say, who seek initiation to these sliddery rites are liable to be left in the dark. Being tardy getting to the hill has often nagged me and truly rousing efforts were made to rectify the fault, especially with the necessity of late to outflank what feels like a typical weekend sales rush to the most popular climbs.

But old vices, these masters of so frightful mien, die hard. Other uneasy recidivists might be equally consoled to know that the latest American research in human chronobiology suggests that our manual dexterity and physical endurance reach a peak, so to speak, in the late afternoon and evening. We might have guessed years ago when so many best walks and hardest climbs were only accomplished on the verge (sometimes the affront) of closing time.

Ian McWhiter and Brian Barr don crampons for the enticing passage of 'Boomerang Gully' on Stob Coire nan Lochan.

Some of the finest and steepest rock climbing in Scotland can be found on the great E-Buttress of Aonach Dubh. A lone climber in the airy No. 4 Gully surveys the main cliff which faces westward to Glencoe village, Loch Leven and Ardgour. Climbing 'Hee-Haw' on E-Buttress (above) gives an impressive taste of the glen's rare mountain atmosphere and diversity.

Overleaf: Derek Lloyd surmounts the notorious pinnacles on the traverse of Aonach Eagach, the notched ridge. The winter itinerary is not commended for novices and the route should be approached with respect at all seasons.

Coast-to-coast charity walker Anne Wakeling takes a break on the Lairigmor stretch of the West Highland Way above Kinlochleven.

A hand placed on chaste rock, an axe struck into frozen crystal at the start of an icy exploration – while safely roped to a competent friend – are mountain quests surely not too difficult to communicate to those a shade more down to earth. Going freely, unencumbered by ropes or other items of protection as many of the adept do now and then, is a new dimension entirely and harder to explain even to oneself. And notably when married, with a family. What is it so many have come to find in the wilderness? Is it atavism, the ancestral hunter divested in a blink of historic time of his freedom and the untamed lands; of the chase, the cave and the dancing shadows? Perhaps modern urban society has swept down like Attila on civilisation.

A few climb solo from choice or the lack of a partner. Only to decorous limits in my case. Others move closer to the edge, depending on conscience, nerve and ability. Still, it baffles me. Forays into the esoteric art are not definitive or recommended. Maybe there is an inert need now and then to test self-reliance and deny that discretion is the better part of valour. When expertise and fitness, of course, are ready for the challenge.

Overt risk-taking is mostly condemned, but the fact that more than 100,000 people of all ages are killed, maimed and hurt each year on Britain's roads is apparently no driving deterrent. Single-handed yachts persons gain high public regard for their achievements at sea. So the lone exploits of South Tyrolean, Reinhold Messner, first mountaineer to bag all 14 Himalayan giants over 8,000 metres and the oxygen-free solo ascent of Everest by Stephen Venables of England, deserve no less. It is our nature to push out the boat, or the space probe. Shrewd enough by now not to make the same mistake more than half-a-dozen times, I grasped at last the concept that where risks are low, so are rewards. Once the idea had ignited, it slung me out into the rarefied environment I inhabit today.

Slipping the dog's collar of a political desk and the regular trade union wrangles of a Glasgow journal, I bade farewell to a cushy income,

Two Liverpool lads embrace the spectacular winter landscape of the glen from Meall Dearg, one of two Munros on Aonach Eagach.

Kinlochleven has magnificent mountain scenery and many fine walks. The season opens with a roar – the advent of the annual Six-Day Motorcycle Trial. Innes Sutherland (above) a local bike enthusiast once ran the weather gauntlet of the Lairigmor, commuting the rugged, 12-mile trail daily to Fort William.

expenses and a meagre Renfrewshire mortgage by present standards. With my wife, three young sons and two beagles I found sanctuary in remotest Argyll. Alaska, it seemed then. My aim was to survive on mountain photo-journalism mainly, a risk venture but not pure spontaneity.

It began with my dad, William R. Thomson, I suppose. A city engineer with reddish hair and a quiet wit, he had been a keen amateur wrestler but quit in shock when a close friend and Scottish bantam champion, Dan McNiven, died in an accident on the mat. It was common in the Depression years of the 1930s for some Glasgow families

A tourist coach enters the Gorge whose falls flow and ebb with the spring snow melt, summer drought and autumn monsoon.

A stone bridge on the old Tyndrum-Glencoe road constructed by Thomas Telford, circa. 1810. Queen Victoria picnicked nearby.

to camp through the summer in Glen Ashdale on Arran, the rugged Firth of Clyde isle favoured by walkers and climbers. Dad would settle mum, my sister and two older brothers there and cycle to and from the city at weekends.

Years on, I would meet veteran clubmen who recalled the slim, ginger-bred man tucked in their slipstream on his Rudge roadster laden with a week's tenting provisions, churning uphill and down across Renfrewshire en route to Ardrossan ferry. He loved the outdoors, the sculpt of a horse much as I appreciate a cliff, and a dram. He bought each of his four sons in turn a lightweight bike, with the stricture that our wheels were to be aimed often out of town, for fun, fresh air and scenic admiration. A bike was the cheapest and usually quickest mode of urban transport and I soon knew not only the city, but much of Central and the West of Scotland.

Achnacon, a former farmhouse acquired by the National Trust for Scotland, is attached to the leishman mountain rescue research centre. Above, the rhyolite walls and gullies of Aonach Dubh west-face warm to the evening sun.

This solitary boulder commands a height on the old Telford road above Allt na Reigh, the stream of the clearing.

then a trot and ultimately like three demented Seb Coes in line, racing for the River Nevis footbridge. As a mildly ambitious junior bike racer, I had never anticipated beery hillmen of such athleticism.

A year later in 1959 came my first winter encounter with Britain's premier mountain, known affectionately in Lochaber as the Big Bad Ben. The *Scottish Daily Express* sent me to keep vigil over New Year, after a series of accidents. All was quiet and days of boredom were lifted with an outing in new boots and deep snow to the halfway lochan. Larry Lyons, the photographer, excused himself from the two-man expedition, intoning from behind a charged glass that we could be the casualties we so patiently expected.

My early-picture taking was spasmodic but induced a later respect for talented photographers, a bent not quite universal then among Albion Street's coterie of reporters. The crafts are strictly segregated on the national press. Only fleetingly did I cross the lines over the years, once for a spell with the *East Kent Mercury* in Deal.

Though Ben Nevis was still a novelty, I already knew the haunting fastness of Glencoe. It was often battled with on epic weekends or bike tours to Skye and the North West. Leaning into the glen's inevitable westerly, under rolling grey cloud, it was a wearysome sprachle at the end of the 90-mile-long and winding road from Ibrox.

I would come camping later, by car and the fast Bonneville 650cc motorcycle inherited for a while from a feature-writer friend, Duncan McNicol, then recovering from a serious road accident. Captivated by the mountains, the concept of actually living, working and climbing among them took years of gestation. A decade, to be precise.

Then in 1971 the pugnacious Lancastrian Don Whillans arrived in Glasgow to publicise his gripping autobiography: the portrait of a remarkable rock climber and Alpine and Himalayan mountaineer. As a leader writer and regular book reviewer with the *Evening Citizen*, I wandered down to the publisher's buffet lunch to meet Joe Brown's equally legendary mate. A man of modest stature, he had a lion's heart.

Rescuers recover a young climber (top left) killed on Buachaille Etive Mor. But the mountain sometimes forgives. A casualty (above) is winched into an RAF helicopter after a technical stretcher lift, Hamish MacInnes attending, below Rannoch Wall.

Previous page Loch Achtriochtan shimmers under bulky Aonach Dubh and Bidean nam Bian – viewed from Am Bodach on the spectacular, notched ridge.

The Lochan under the Pap is a
favourite walk of visitors. Lord
Strathcona created the extended
garden for his Canadian wife.

Glencoe also offers relaxing days.
A young oarsman (above) takes to
Loch Leven off Tighphuirst, the
pierhouse. Cycling is a favoured
 activity in Glencoe and around
 Loch Leven. Bryan Anderson pedals
the single track road at Clachaig.

Hamish MacInnes, not unsung either in his own country, was there for moral support. Their bond was strong for Don had ensured Hamish's survival on an epic ascent of the Bonatti Pillar above Chamonix in 1958 when a stray stone from a rockfall fractured his skull. Don seemed a tinge subdued in this literary sphere, sipped lager and disposed of a platter of oysters like a man posting letters.

The ex-Salford plumber's dry wit was perhaps curbed on that occasion but its sharp edge was amusingly evident in the few cryptic postcards he would send in an erratic correspondence. A touch of black humour surfaced at the slide lecture I arranged (Whillans' word would be, botched) in Govan for Don and Hamish in 1974. Describing the retrieval of an Everest fatality, suspended overnight on the rope after a fall, he told his audience, 'I knew he were dead. I tapped with me hammer and he rang loud and clear.'

His acid genius is preserved in an alleged riposte to a pretentious German at a Himalayan base camp. Extracting himself from some celebratory mates at the close of a radio report on a vital World Cup clash, a jovial Teuton advised Whillans and Co that West Germany had just beaten England at her national sport. Not famed for cementing friendships, the Lancastrian returned, 'Aye . . . but as I recall, England has already defeated Germany twice at her national game.' The man who once warned partner Joe Brown in a television replay of a classic Llanberis climb, 'Here I come, 14-stone of fighting flab,' was deservedly a cult figure and died, aged 52, in bed.

A lucky outcome of the publisher's lunch was an invitation from Hamish to sample the admirable winter climbing courses he ran with fellow instructors in Glencoe. It turned out to be a brilliant March week, the mountains were luminous and my series of articles were well projected. I wrote of the first day's route, 'Evening Citizen', a grade IV climb on lofty Stob Coire nan Lochan, 'For the first time I am alone. I look out over the snowfield a thousand miles below. I can hear the silence of the place and it is sublime. It is a particularly beautiful day because I am frightened.'

A croft cottage at Carnoch. The main village street looks to the Pap of Glencoe, a popular if strenuous climb. It gives a wide panorama.

The Macdonald memorial (top left) to those massacred in 1692 at Carnoch attracts streams of visitors throughout the year.

The Three Sisters make impressive impact on the descent to Glen Coe from Buachaille Etive Beag.

Ex-police sergeant Kenny MacKenzie, co-founder of the Search and Rescue Dog Assoc., with four-legged friend Echo.

My feelings have changed little. From that winter of 1971 I was determined to migrate to the West Highlands and in November three years later moved with my family to a temporary refuge in Kinlochleven, and a year later to our present ex-ferryman's cottage. The beagles died of old age and hard running and were replaced with Gemma, a springer-collie cross just as enamoured of Glencoe's rare liberty. More than half-a-dozen cats have come and gone, and two remain.

Brought up in Glasgow's busy west end, Ann is today a Glencoe devotee. How could anyone fond of nature be otherwise? For years a couple of roe deer fed at dawn around our back garden. Barn owls share the woodland mice with our felines. Three pairs of grey herons nest nearby. Eider ducks flock and cormorants dive in Loch Leven just below the house, and oystercatchers promenade on the shore. Buzby buzzard keeps his seat on the telephone pole when I drive for the paper and in season, curlews and peesweep fly in the adjacent field. We have seen sea otters at four local locations and the daddy of them all just escaped the car's front wheels as we drove to Ballachulish. Golden eagles float in the glen and ravens wheel the crags. As we walk the dog at dusk, red deer hinds emerge from the Lairig Gartain and graze under Buachaille Etive Beg and heading home, a stag party crops the grass at Achtriochtan.

I write and take pictures for most of Britain's national daily and Sunday newspapers, for magazines and other publications and for radio and television. Without my 15 years' professional experience behind me, viability at best would have been doubtful.

Adapting in a sense to the crofting tradition, I diversified, sometimes guiding clients on the hills, taking pictures when the chance came for future outlets. Photography became a vital source of journalistic income as I had anticipated and I strove to improve, eventually winning an important section in a major Scottish press picture competition, with a mountain rescue sequence. A first and last foray in that domain.

The great runs of mackerel on Loch Leven are wonders of the past but young folk can still wish and fish at Tighphuirst.

Previous page: The east face of Aonach Dubh lurches imposingly above the A82. Its difficult climbs were the subject of a recent live outdoor BBC TV spectacular. Joe Brown and Jackie Antoine climbed 'Freak-Out' and Dave Cuthbertson and Murray Hamilton, 'Spacewalk' the difficulty of the extreme routes enhanced by persistent rain.

Much of my work takes me out of the area of Ballachulish and Glencoe. There are articles on mountain, climbing and skiing subjects but social interest and environmental issues predominate. In the course of things, I have ranged from Orkney to Cornwall, Aberdeen to St Kilda. I have written at times about mountain accidents in the glen and on Ben Nevis, hoping the dissemination of hard facts will reduce the often simple slips and errors of judgement that lead to injury, tragedy and misery for next of kin.

I have been a member of Glencoe Mountain Rescue Team since 1975 and though call-outs tend to remain on average around 30 a year with up to 10 walkers and climbers killed, this near-static rate is remarkable considering the mountain invasions of today, especially in winter.

On many fine days I have escaped to the local hills with my cameras and come back to the light rebuff that it was time I got myself a real job. The pictures here are the evidence of my good intent on these countless jaunts. Most of the colour shots were gathered at random on mountain walks and climbs and the black and white as newspaper and other assignments. I have not attempted to present a comprehensive view of Glencoe, simply to 'expose' the film that has accumulated in my personal archive.

Though my income hardly matches the rates on national feature or picture desks, any urge to adandon the glen's good life for urban affluence is usually easily resisted. Henry Thoreau found in this two years at Walden pond in Concord, Massachusetts, that wealth relates to the things you can afford to leave alone.

Though photo-journalism in the Highlands can at times give a sense of isolation, again like the Concord sage I discovered that often there is no friend so companionable as solitude. Or so appreciative of our moods as silence. If ever I was seriously tempted to waver, this dispersed after I broke my neck in a car accident returning from Saturday skiing with my son in 1980.

Graham escaped unhurt to my eternal gratitude but in the whiplash shunt after skidding on black ice, my neck was dislocated and three cervicles fractured. Removed carefully from the car by friends, I was soon in the finest professional care. Local hospital superintendent Mr Iain Campbell had me rapidly transferred on a stryker stretcher to the Royal Infirmary in Edinburgh, and Scotland's leading consultant neurosurgeon. I was to recover quickly and completely to ski, cycle and climb again and with minimal nerve impingement.

Anxious about my livelihood and family, I virtually signed myself out in 10 days. Though strongly drugged with steroids to subdue the spinal chord, I felt I had to work. Ron Anderson, executive editor of the *Glasgow Herald* who published most of my features, thoughtfully offered me a desk in Glasgow while I recuperated. I fear I produced nothing of any account. This generosity and the many local kindnesses Ann and my sons experienced during that awkward period brought it home that despite earlier appearances, we are never out on a limb in Glencoe.

The River Coe cloe to the watershed. Below is The Study, or Anvil, a flat rock where Queen Victoria lunched with John Brown.

CHAPTER THREE

The Road to Rannoch

Loch Tulla (left) is viewed to good effect just before the renovated concrete bridge at Black Mount. Lone skier Ron Weir tests the 'Thrombosis' piste, Glencoe.

BLACK MOUNT, THE portal to Glencoe, swells above Loch Tulla just beyond the clachan of Bridge of Orchy on the sweeping A82. The road north curves up around the green eminence of Glas Bheinn and allows fine retrospects of the big Achaladair escarpment and the West Highland Railway dwarfed below. The line swings north-east from the road here, its single track forging boldly into a remnant of the once-great Wood of Caledon. South is the bulky Bheinn an Dothaid, the hill of scorching, and a comparatively pastoral Glen Orchy. More distantly across the refulgent loch to the west, the trident tops of Ben Starav rise above some courtiers, a view enhanced at sunset.

Near the summit of the pass at more than 1,000 ft a seemingly frail sapling, the Rannoch Rowan, weirdly splits a lone glacial boulder, It serves wells on the left of the road as a milestone to the rugged vista ahead. A barbican of peaks rises around the stony flanks of Clach Leathad (or Clachlet) 3,602 ft, and the all-embracing Coire Ba which is Scotland's largest natural cauldron. Westward across ragged Lochan an h-Achlaise, the waters of the hollow, the Black Mount hills fill the skyline.

From Stob Ghabhar, or goat peak, they reach to Meall a'Bhuiridh's ski slopes and the great ridge-tent outline of Sron na Creise at Glen Etive on the edge of the porphyritic ring fault. This is the north-east boundary of the cold magma that gives capricious Glencoe her rare climbing quality and scenic grandeur. But before the fast highway begins its impressive descent to Buachaille Etive Mor, it is the Moor of Rannoch that catches the speculative eye with its quiet air of desolation.

The moor sweeps away right to the remote outpost of Schiehallion, the Perthshire stack from which the astronomer royal, Dr Neville Maskelyne, made observations in 1774 that helped ascertain the mean density of the planet. Rannoch Moor, in effect, is a 60-square-mile rockery of moss, heather, marsh grass and strewn boulders. It lies 1,000 ft and more above sea-level and slopes only gently around myriad

A luxury taxi service from Clachaig Inn! Dave Clemm of PLM, the most experienced mountain fliers in the North, awaits television clients who have dropped in to the hotel for lunch.

Another popular means of arrival, motorcycle, was the regular transport of top Glasgow climber, John Cunningham renowned for spectacular crashes en route.

From the ski slopes of Meall a'Bhuiridh, Coire Ba, Loch Tulla and Glenorchy (right) bathe in luminous light.

Lochan Ur, or the new loch, in Glen Etive reflects on the perfect glacial valley between the two Buachailles.

Opposite page: A new moon rises over Schiehallion (top) and Rannoch Moor. The moor's lochans from Buachaille Etive Mor (lower right) and the view to Clachlet across Lochan na h-Achlaise.

blue lochans and its few larger lochs. From Kingshouse in the west, a rough road to the shooting lodge at Black Corries extends another two or three miles then runs as a broken trail a farther ten miles to the B846 at Rannoch Station on the West Highland line to Fort William.

The walk and its arresting views are better going from east to west, in late spring, when the snows still give a sheen to the crests of Black Mount and the Buachaille. Care should be taken in winter, for experienced gangrels have lost their lives in the wilder reaches, caught out by the abrupt squalls and blizzards to which the Highlands are prone due to the Atlantic drift.

The desert swath from Rannoch south again to Black Mount is trackless, apart from the railway line winding farther to the east by the Waters of Tulla to Bridge of Orchy and eventually Glasgow. The iron road might never have existed if seven Victorians who set out in 1889 to check construction costs and land values for the promoters had been a shade less lucky in their epic, midwinter traverse from Loch Treig to Inveroran.

Setting out on January 30 from a lodge on the loch dressed more for a chilly day about town than a 25-mile bog-trot on the bleakest Scottish moor, the party had fractured by midway. Two chose stoically to freeze in the company of the elderly collapsed land agent while the other four pressed on for succour.

The surveyor was the only wayfarer among them who had crossed the moor before. He missed the cottage he aimed for at Gorton and, utterly spent, folded on a wire fence in the dark. Some hours later he awoke to his mission, found the house, alerted a pair of shepherds and quickly re-folded in one of their beds. The icy trio squatting out in the myrtle were located, taken to a bothy at 3 am, warmed and fed. Somewhat revived next day, they were guided to Gorton where the engineer and the lawyer had been extracted from a night's cold comfort behind a rock.

Some bedraggled commandos were duly escorted, one in a cart,

Winter mountaineering on Bidean nam Bian; running the West Highland Way; and grappling with Glencoe's most spectacular scramble, Curved Ridge. Sron na Creise and Meall a'Bhuiridh rise across the River Etive.

to Inveroran. The contractor who had stumbled farther than the rest was recovered en route from a goodly woman's abode. It was three days since the party had left Spean Bridge and on the next, a blizzard blew across the moor.

In seasonal weather, brown trout fishermen and walkers explore the plateau, often by leaps and bounds and mostly from the parking space on the A82 at Loch Ba. Trekking is mainly to the east of elongated Loch Laidon and its sandy inlets where red and black divers are known to swim and golden plover and dunlin nest.

The moor has a varied plant carpet but trees are scarce and confined largely to the islets. Both red and roe deer graze this desolate landscape when the surrounding hills are snow-plastered and are often observed at dawn, or dusk by drivers as they run the gauntlet of the rapid A82. The deer, that is.

If the aim of a walk in the heather is to remain entirely dry-shod, the peaty ground is best left until the drier spells of late May and June. A navigable waterway stretches north-east to the River Gaur and Loch Rannoch, a popular venture for competent canoeists ready at times to haul. Most of the route has been swum, skated in winter and by now may well have been wind-surfed.

Though assumed to take its name from the bracken, Rannoch could have another interpretation. The infernal fern fares better on lower slopes of hills than the moorland. Gaelic has a word, raonach, for a level tract of land or plain country. How better to describe the expansive table that until the end of the last ice age some 9,000 years ago bore the weight of mighty glaciers up to 5,000 ft thick?

Like giants playing chess, the alternating ice eras grinding east at times then west, deposited granite boulders from the moor on the Bidean massif summits and carried others from the Glen Coe heights to Rannoch. In the millennia, water courses were cut, diverted and erased by the terminal moraines from the ice in high corries. An early drainage system rising beyond Glen Tarbert in Ardgour, before the cleavage of

An autumn day in Glen Coe (far left) may open with cloud and showers and close in mellow mood. Winter walks on summits can be diverting. Threat of storm (above left) on Stob Coire Altruin, looking south to Loch Etive, is as rewarding as a spring heatwave on Gearr Aonach (above).

A summit assembly on Bidean
nam Bian is routine, all through
the year. Argyll's highest peak
draws a devoted retinue.

Loch Linnhe, flowed east through Glen Coe and across the moor,
perhaps to debouch much as Loch Laidon and Loch Rannoch do now in
the North Sea.

Choked eventually by glacial debris near Buachaille Etive Beg,
the glen's watershed, the River Coe gradually began to flow west.
Though slowly at first, the eons brough greater erosion and steeper
inclines and the streams raced to merge with the enthusiasm lauded
today.

But the evolution of this wild hinterland on the frontier of Central
Scotland and Lochaber has a grievous aspect. Exposed in the peat hags
of Coir Ba, in the Buachaille lairigs, or passes, and on the moor are the
relics of the great Caledonian forest that once covered 60 per cent of the
country.

The ancient woods of Scotland, the seemingly endless acres of
rich Scots pine, oak, birch, rowan, alder and hazel were systematically
destroyed. All the evidence is there, in the peat bogs and tarns: root and
branch. From the wanton ruin of a magnificent natural and national
asset (less then 10 per cent of the land is wooded today) the world at large
appears to have learned nothing. David Attenborough warns that the
immense tropical rain forests may be gone, at the present rate of
destruction, by 2,000 AD! The whale, the rhino and the elephant are
menaced. A government hunting tally in British Columbia for a single
year, recently, was 20,000 moose, 3,000 black bears and 500 grizzly.

Scotland's wealth of timber was consumed at first by Neolithic
communities clearing the trees for sheep, goats and oxen. Later, the Pics
burned in defence and the Vikings in offence. For more than 2,000 years
the smelting of iron caused massive woodland clearances. Shipbuilding
was equally voracious. Gradually, the shrinking forest could not sustain
its extensive wildlife. Irish and European elk, reindeer, wolves, bears,
wild boar, beavers and the broad-tailed otter were slain or departed.

Wolves enforced regular hunts in the Highlands, up to three
times a year in some rural areas, and by the 17th Century in Sutherland

The gaunt citadel of Bidean nam
Bian. Diamond Buttress is to the
left and Church Door on the right.
Collie's Pinnacle nestles between.

the bounty on the animal even then had risen to a value of more than £6. In less than 100 years the wolf had been eliminated. Charles Dickens and his fellow coach travellers would not have feared it in 1841 when they arrived in the glen on the old Military Road from Tyndrum. The eminent novelist no doubt journeyed with great expectations but found little inspirational to write home about.

Rannoch Moor was its desolate self on a day of mist and driving rain. Boulders loomed from the mirk like tombstones. In a letter, he lamented, 'It had been impossible to keep warm, by any means; even whisky failed. The wind was too piercing even for that. One stage of ten miles, over a place called the Black-Mount, took us two hours and a half to do; and then we came to a lone public called the King's House, at the

King's House Hotel on the fringe of Rannoch Moor. Dorothy Wordsworth on a Highland tour with her brother in 1803, described it thus: 'The house looked respectable at a distance – a large square building, cased in slates to defend it from storms – but when we came close to it the outside forewarned us of the poverty and misery within.'

Previous page: Loch Leven looking to Kinlochleven and the Mamore hills. The loch is mildly spoiled now with a brace of sometimes smelly fish farms and the industrious West Highland town by the fumes of the British Alcan aluminium plant. But industry is vital even here.

A happy casualty is stretchered off the Meall a'Bhuiridh plateau. This magnificent seven (right) under the forceful leadership of Bert Dobbie (second from left) ensured the safety of skiers and evacuated the injured from the slopes for many years.

entrance to Glencoe . . .' Today, the King's House Hotel is a popular watering-hole not just for tourists but a regular clinetele of walkers, climbers and skiers who cavort on the piste of Meall a'Bhuiridh, just across the way.

Dickens and his friends warmed themselves by the inn fire and were quickly served kipper, salmon, broiled fowl, mutton, poached eggs, pancakes, oatcakes, wheaten bread and butter. Of which, he added superfluously, they made a hearty meal. And they followed up with bottles of porter and a toddy.

Things were clearly on the mend at the old horse changehouse

which Dr. Samuel Johnson, an Egon Ronay of his day, curtly dismissed as a noisesome place infested with, what he termed, 'cut-purses'. Climbers who cram the Buachaille Etive Mor by day and the King's House public bar at night clearly uphold a long and loud tradition. When exactly the Hanoverian changehouse was built is not known, but a hostelry of sorts called the Queen's House stood slightly west of the present location around the turn of the 16th Century. Military road builders often gave their fixed quarters a royal designation. Soon ordinary travellers as well as soldiers making for Fort William (after William of Orange) were changing to fresh horses there.

A Captain Basil Hall tells of coming across early roadmen maintaining the zig-zags on the Devil's Staircase, a route often credited to General Wade, but like most West Highland ways built in fact around 1750, by his successor Major, and later General, Edward Caulfeild.

Sixteen men occupied a caravan, 'like a ship of the mountains,' plying on the road with cartloads of gravel and stones, a style updated to winter gritting and snowploughing on the A82 now.

A fine observer of the antiquated scene was Charles Weld, who on a tour in 1860 took the last coach of the season from Fort William to Loch Lomond. No other passengers expected, he noted that, 'Everybody considered he had full licence to get drunk.' How the coach running erratically on whisky got through Glen Coe was a mystery. Weld walked the last stretch to King's House arriving long before the vehicle reeled up.

Dying for a drink took a new depth of meaning, though, during the building of the Blackwater dam for the British Aluminium factory at Kinlochleven at the turn of the century. An Irish navvy or two collapsed and expired traversing the Devil's Staircase in blizzards heading for a tot. No Scottish inn has a more fulsome testimonial.

White Corries' skiers endure a plod from the main chair to the plateau (above left). T-bar uplift terminates at a vista.

CHAPTER FOUR

The Glades of Etive

Young skiers poised on the edge of
Coire Ba and the panorama to
Achallader, Beinn an Dothiadh
and Loch Tulla. Early-season
means a tow-freeze (above).

Jumping for joy. In Eddie the Eagle mode? Meall a'Bhuiridh has a wide range of runs and space to ski on an off-day.

MEALL A'BHUIRIDH, THE hill of bellowing, refers to the red deer stags warning off rivals from their harems of hinds gathered in summer around the ski slopes and the more secluded Cam Ghleann, below the piste. Some veterans of the hill allege that the name came from their own yells of delight at finding such exhilarating winter sport so close to home. Glasgow and district skiers, only 90 miles or so from the glen, contributed enormously over the years to the development of the popular resort. And not a few from the Edinburgh area also made a deep impression, as they say, on the hill.

Early downhillers favoured Black Mount and Coire Ba long before the tows and chairs went up on Meall a'Bhuiridh (say, Melavoory). Keen to broaden their outdoor expertise or simply have fun in these snow-swept mountains, many would trudge at weekends up the long east ridge of Clach Leathad. Chris Lyon, long-term president of Glencoe Ski Club, the most active racing and recreational concern with its own plateau hut and a lodge at Bridge of Orchy, recalls shouldering skis and slogging 6,000 ft uphill in a day, just for the joy of bashing down again into Coire Ba.

Strongly to the fore on those pioneering slides was the Creagh Dhu Club and its matey opposition, the Lomond Mountaineering Club. For years after the war they had caught the same Campbeltown milk lorry from the city, or shared a bus for their active weekends in Glencoe. A regular doss was the deserted Ba Cottage on the old drove road from Kingshouse to the celebrated cattle tryst of Inveroran. Poachers, however, fell foul of the local estate and as a punative measure a keeper fired the roof of the isolated bothy. Peeved but undaunted, the mountain fraternity extracted timbers from the burned house and relocated themselves beneath a tarpaulin on the site of a bygone fank and cheesehouse at what is now the White Corries car park.

This was the founding of the present ski rescue patrol and the Meall a'Bhuiridh workforce, for the Clydeside shipyard skills of these

Chris Lyon, a stalwart of Glencoe skiing and the local ski club.

accomplished hillmen were ever in demand. The first Scottish Ski Club tow of 1956 was a hand-rope driven by a petrol engine removed from a Chevrolet car driven up to the slopes. Chris Lyon said he could not remember if the owner was consulted.

In need of venture capital, the SSC approached the merchant banker owner of Black Mount Estate and in 1960 White Corries Limited began to operate the first chairlift and T-bar tows in Britain. It was a modestly audacious enterprise then and has never looked back, despite the frights of recent mild winters. And it was to prove a prototype for more ambitious projects carried by some of its own Clydeside artisans to Cairngorm and Glenshee. Though soon outclassed by the scale, all-electric Swiss gear and sophisticated catering of these centres and now grossly overshadowed by the elegant, gondola-served facility at Aonach Mor on the threshold of Ben Nevis, Glencoe's scintillating skiing is hard to beat.

No other Scots centre has quite the diversity of runs for the discerning skier as Meall a'Bhuiridh, though the outlook from Aonach Mor to Loch Eil, Loch Linnhe and the Western Isles rivals the glen's views across Rannoch Moor, Buachaille Etive Mor and to the Big Bad Ben. White Corries lives up well to the contention that skiing is a grand family sport with descents to match every taste and all levels of skill.

Open usually only for long weekends and the Easter holiday fortnight, the compact resort has little scope to expand and is easily overwhelmed at busy periods. Space reaches a premium above 1,200 skiers and the rescue patrol becomes active with collision accidents. There are 11 varied runs, from the sheer Flypaper to the sweeping Etive Glades, each with its own ambiance. On a brilliant spring day when the throng is incarcerated in employment or inexplicably diverted elsewhere, Meall a'Bhuiridh's svelte powder and panoramas make an idyll rarely found this side of Valhalla.

Such days are scarce, however, and hedonism needs to be earned. For 30 years there were no toilets above the lower ticket office,

White Corries breeds future race talent.

Loch Achtriochtan in the heart of Glen Coe (right). The still waters beneath Aonach Dubh and Aonach Eagach soften the scene.

The walk up to Coire nan Lochan from the A82 near Achtriochtan gives entrancing views to the Aonach Eagach ridge.

which might explain many crossed skis at Glencoe. Squalls often put a damper on things and radar alone penetrates mountain mist. Gales can play havoc with tows and chairs and some east breezes have enough refrigeration to quell an Eskimo, or Inuit. Yet happy families who might otherwise be huddled round an urban fireside, freeze to their chair seats, join frigid tow queues then skid numbly down Mugs' Alley for a reviving cuppa. Ptarmigan in their winter white and the ubiquitous snow bunting shuffle and flit, pecking warily at chance picnic crumbs.

All standards are catered for at White Corries, and there is a ski school and hire service. The small plateau caff in which I have imbibed many a glass of white wine (invariably my own because the hill as yet is unlicensed) has been newly pine-panelled, extended and finally toileted. Plans are afoot to erect a double chairlift to replace the single that staunchly hoisted countless skiers and summer sightseers to the heights. And not a few walkers take a hitch to save their legs for the excursion and superlative views over Rannoch Moor on the trek to and from Clach Leathad and Stob Ghabhar in the south. But such baroque ornaments at White Corries are mere decadence to the old trailblazers of the Creag Dhu and Lomond MC.

Sometimes, for a newspaper picture, I have skied the hill with friends on Midsummer's Day when the late snow allowed, but the season proper ends just after Easter. Then the greying hardpack gets the brunt of the sun even on these northern slopes, and a big melt starts. Descending in the chair, the cascading Allt nan Giubhas, or pine burn, wafts just a tincture of nascent summer and if the mists drift on the lochans of Rannoch, the tawny moor can seem like Africa.

The stream tumbles loudly through the heather on warm-pink beds beyond Black Rock Cottage, a bothy of the Ladies' Scottish Climbing Club formed in 1908. It joins the River Etive, which rises in the Black Corries, before it flows beneath the newly renovated, 1935 concrete road bridge at Kingshouse. Due west across the heath the sentinel of Stob Dearg, the red peak of Buachaille Etive Mor, towers impressively over the A82.

Black Rock Cottage on the old military road from Bridge of Orchy to Kingshouse.

Now the shallow brown waters gather width and momentum as they run south-west, parallel with the single-track road down Glen Etive, a 13-mile trip to the eponymous loch and its sadly dwindling rural community. Wildly attractive with deep swimming pools, rocky bluffs and chasms and a remarkable ridge walk, the glen and Loch Etive have much active outdoor interest.

In the early 1950s, the winding, undulating road served more than 50 people. The Department of Agriculture farmed 3,000 sheep and Donald MacArthur another 2,000 at Dalness farm. He and his wife Mary, the local primary teacher, left in 1961 for health reasons and the sheep and their tups, or rams, were sold. Soon the blackface ewes of the DoA were also cleared from behind Bidean nan Bian and around Ben Starav.

If Glen Coe is the weeping glen then Glen Etive mourns in sympathy. Shepherds and stalkers duly departed with their families and the population declined to the fragile 16 who live there today. At one stage the stone primary school taught only the son and daughter of a local keeper. Maybe this gave an even chance of being top of the class, but the small primary in turn closed its doors and the pupils commuted 20 miles to Glencoe or stayed at the Lochaber High School hostel.

The striking mansion that emerges from the larches just below some fine trout and salmon pools, is Dalness House, in the vale of the waterfalls. It is a second residence of a cousin of another absentee landlord, London merchant banker Robin Fleming, owner of Black Mount and Glen Etive Estates and chairman of White Corries Limited. Stalking is carried on at these glen properties, but employment is at a minimum. The Forestry Commission is another extensive owner here and there are murmurs of the trees being sold off with the land.

A new lodge was built beside the old Glenetive House but is barely discernable among the roadside oaks. For a decade, craftsman forester Dave Bonnett has farmed up to 35 red deer, but the future of the project now seems uncertain.

A bleak winter's day after heavy snowfall above The Study has its own intrinsic beauty.

At the farm buildings here, Jock and Morag Fraser have lived for 30 years, he as chief stalker now on the estate and his wife the postmistress serving summer visitors, climbers and the small local community from a tidy desk in her front room. My brother Bill was friendly for the same period with their near-neighbour, Charlie Cattanach, the local water-bailie for many years and a character-and-a-half. Before he died, Charlie cut and shaped me a hazel crummock, or shepherds crook, so that after my car accident I had always, 'a sturdy companion on the hill,' as he put it. I have never used the prized possession.

Whether the Glen Coe tops are snow-dusted, gowned in white velvet or rock-bare, this scene remains indelible to visitors. Enveloped beneath Gearr Aonach and Aonach Dubh are the ancient moraines from Coire Cabhail and Coire Lochan.

The River Etive winds its gracious way between reddish rock banks and rowans, meandering to steep falls and through mysterious pools that are excellent for swimming in high summer.

The twisting glen road terminates at the delapidated, wooden estate pier on Loch Etive. Today it serves only the gulls, though a boat cruises with tourists almost to Kinlochetive twice a day in summer. They nest and rear their young in the hollows of the outer pier posts, attacking anyone who swings out on the rickety structure. Gymnastics are best confined to the sweeping slabs exposed on the granite bastion of Beinn Trilleachan, the oystercatcher peak, on the west shore of the loch.

These soaring stone acres have a network of delicate climbs (and often a profusion of midges) reaching to 800 ft and more. Most are above the very severe standard and require a subtle approach and the coolest of nerve. From the coffin stone at the foot of the slabs, the view to Ben Starav, a popular Munro just opposite, and south across the sparkling loch to the great cirque of Cruachan, is spell-binding. Both east and west shores of Loch Etive can be walked. Another fine approach to the area is made via Victoria Bridge at Loch Tulla through Glen Kinglass by Loch Dochart to Ardmaddy. Much of it is by Land Rover track and ideal on foot and mountain bike, but the lochside stretch to Kinlochetive, though dramatic, can be purgatory.

Ard, or airde, is a height and madadh-ruadh, a fox. From the confluence of the River Kinglass with Loch Etive at Ardmaddy Bay the trail south by a footbridge is to Glen Noe and Taynuilt on the A85 from Oban to Tyndrum, and so back to Bridge of Orchy and Victoria Bridge. Northward, the nine shoreline miles to Coileitir bridge and the Glen Etive road is arduous and an affliction for cyclists due to the relentless watercourses off Ben Starav. A bike is best because the memorable 40-mile tour requires transport from the glen back to your start, or a hitch which is slim.

Many make this beautiful circuit and with varied solutions. Some have minor epics. Like the motorcycle trialist who, demented at the drainage channels to be crossed, drove his machine in frustration into the loch and awaited aid from Glencoe Mountain Rescue Team! And I recall the once-sleek racing cyclist who lost his usual aristocratic

The Etive slabs of fine granite give superlative friction climbs of unusual challenge. And grand views of Cruachan and Glen Coe.

These Highland garrons in Glen Etive were used for years to bring the red deer down from the hill after a day's stalking.

David Bonnett, (right) a craftsman forester, has farmed a small red deer herd in the glen for a number of years.

bearing. After lengthy self-indulgence he made an ill-starred comeback with friends on this outing, slumped badly and was deposited for the 80-mile drive back to Glasgow on a pile of bikes in the rear of a van. There was an occasional mutter from the otherwise comatose lump which implied that a career on two wheels had been terminated.

Glen Etive has several approaches from the east and gives scenic routes west and north to Glen Coe, by the Bealach Fhionnghaill to Achnacon and through the lairigs of Gartain and Eilde that divide the two Buachailles from each other and from Bheinn Fhada. Bridge of Orchy, with an admirable hotel and modern bunkhouse used extensively by West Highland Way walkers, is a commendable base.

The road from here west of the River Orchy to Inveroran ends, as a car route, just after Victoria Bridge at Forest Lodge. It goes on as a right of way on the old Caulfeild road to a 1,400 ft ridge of Meall a'Bhuiridh, and usually a winter snowdrift, before the descent to Black Rock Cottage and Kingshouse. This walk, or mountain bike ride, skirts the Coire Ba. It gives access by foot from Ba Bridge to a fine pass, the Bealach Fuar-chathaidh, between Aonach Mor and Clach Leathad. And drops form its magnificent setting down to the lodge at Alltchaorun mainly by the south bank of the burn, then the north at a footbridge to reach the Glen Etive road over a final hurdle – a locked gate on the River Etive bridge. Again, some means of return transport is required.

CHAPTER FIVE

Classic Climbs

The first steep moves (left) on the classic climb, Agag's Groove, on Rannoch Wall, Buachaille Etive Mor. An airy situation (above) on the edge of the wall.

Approaching the crux of a Very
Severe test-piece, Brevity Crack,
on east-face North Buttress. A
steep and technical crack move is
followed by an awkward shelf.

Alex Small, one of the bold trio
who pioneered Agag's Groove.

RANNOCH WALL IS an intimidating, 300 ft rampart on the south-east face of Buachaille Etive Mor. From directly below on Curved Ridge, one of the country's finest and Glen Coe's most frequented scrambles, the cliff's pale red porphyry gives a scary, holdless impression. Actually to climb on the edifice gives a quite different aspect today, assuming you don't get vertigo. The fine-grained rock is clean cut, the ledges wide as a bus stance and the environ, perhaps exposed but safe.

The wall's most celebrated line, Agag's Groove, was pristine and enigmatic in 1936, the crux steep, moist and dirty. Hamish Hamilton, an ebullient Glasgow salesman, removed his sandshoes for the awkward bit and trusted to his woolly socks. With merely the protection of a rope and no running belays, the threesome who made the first ascent of this now classic route, more than half a century ago, was irredeemably bold as brass. And to snatch what in due course was to become Scotland's most popular and renowned v.diff.climb,they had to outpace a rival party.

Alex Small, a retired head teacher and the former Rolls-Royce

Chris Bonington made impact in Glen Coe.

engineer, Alex Anderson, made up that forceful trio. Now 80 and resident in darkest Crieff, Small's salient memory of a first attempt on the climb is being resolutely feart. But a strong hint soon after that initial retreat that stalwarts of the Junior Mountaineering Club of Scotland, W H Murray, W M Mackenzie and others had similar ambitions, that fine August morning, drove them back to the dawn wall of Crowberry Ridge. Friendly, and sometimes not so amicable competition was always a climbing spur – since Whymper conquered the Matterhorn – even if an early literary genre implied otherwise.

Glen Coe was ripe for exploitation as a rock and ice arena when William Naismith wrote in 1889 to the *Glasgow Herald* suggesting what was soon to evolve as the Scottish Mountaineering Club. Collie, Solly and Collier made the first assault on the north face of the Buachaille in 1894. Naismith's own original line on Crowberry Ridge came two years later and with the harder, pioneering Direct Route by the ardent

The Clydebank shipwright who perpetrated Brevity Crack, Pat Walsh (above) now crofts at Isle Ornsay, Skye. He left many such teasers in his wake.

Youthful enthusiasm of Colin Barr
on Curved Ridge (top).
Dave Cooper strides into the sunset
on Beinn a'Bheithir (above).
Crux of Robin Smith's tense
classic, The Big Top (right).

Keeping cool on the extreme line,
Lady Jane, on Aonach Dubh(left).
Below the icefall on No. 6 Gully,
Aonach Dubh (top).
Approach to Curved and Crowberry
Ridges on the Buachaille (above).

Lakeland brothers George and Ashley Abraham in 1900, the game, as the Victorians expressed it, was afoot.

Glen Coe, and the Buachaille in particular, played an influential part in the advancement of Scottish climbing on rock and ice. Even now the glen ensures to a greater extent that national achievements remain not too detached from the outrageous, fingery athleticism of youth in England and Wales.

The now classic winter ascent of Crowberry Gully by Harold Raeburn in 1909 was a token of things and characters to come. Bill Murray, who wrote a vivid account of his climbs, *Mountaineering in Scotland*, while a POW in Germany inspired a whole generation, Chris Bonington included. He picked the lock of the rock in Clachaig Gully and chipped his way up the ice of Deep-Cut Chimney on Stob Coire nam Beith in 1939. His spell in the freezer draws the same tense combatants even today.

John Cunningham, a Glasgow wrestling champion and Creagh Dhu guru devised with Yvon Chouinard and Hamish MacInnes a curved axe and front-point crampon technique that led the climbing world into a new winter era. His quality rock climbs on the Buachaille and elsewhere, before his tragic drowning at Gogarth, Anglesey, remain testpieces from the 1950s – Whortleberry Wall, Carnivore, Gallows.

Hamish MacInnes put up a plethora of summer and winter routes in the glen, often with his students, and lifted the prized Raven's Gully, an ice classic in 1953 with Bonington. Jimmy Marshall, the witty and charismatic Edinburgh architect still drifts wraith-like around the cliffs and is known to sink a pint at King's House. The ubiquitous ringmaster perpetuates his name with technical, stylish climbs like Trapeze on the big E buttress of Aonach Dubh, and Unicorn on Stob Coire nan Lochan. Mentor to both Dougal Haston and Robin Smith, young Scots to rank among Britain's finest mountaineers before their deaths on far flung peaks, he truly deserves the epithet, master craftsman.

Smith, an Edinburgh philosophy student, drew a thin but

Ever-innovative, Hamish MacInnes finds a mountain bike the ideal machine for long photo treks in the hills.

Edinburgh master craftsman
James Marshall set a remarkable
climbing pace in Glencoe and on
Ben Nevis.

indelible line up the Buachaille's Slime Wall in 1958. Martin Boysen,
one of England's best long-term technicians knew his capacity to scare.
Of Shibboleth, a 550 ft extreme airing, he wrote, 'The process of
climbing is mercifully totally absorbing, but I felt fearful; lost on the
wall, with nothing to go for. No runners relieved the tension of climbing.
Each move is hard, although no move is harder than the next, but as the
rope runs out in a single sweep the sense of exposure increases
terrifyingly.'*

Well to the fore in the glen's more recent demonology is another
capital product, Dave Cuthbertson. His winter unravelling of the
complex Slime Wall rock climb, Guerdon Grooves, along with some
tenuous and strenuous escapades on Gone With the Wind and
Romantic Reality, both taxing extremes, are very much in the Smithian
mould. A compact mountain enclave, Glencoe has extensive ice culture
and rock architecture to offer the world, even if Coleridge did disclaim it,
in the grip of the ague.

Hard Rock, Ken Wilson,
Hart–Davis MacGibbon

CHAPTER SIX

A Gilded Carnivore

Walking to Bealach Dearg, the red pass, in the Lost Valley.
Entry in winter (left) at The Boulder to Lost Valley, or Coire Gabhail, the corrie of capture.

GLENCOE'S INTRINSIC QUALITY is that so much diversity of landscape should be crammed into such a localised domain. Amid high rocky profiles there are shadowed glens and sunlit moors. Bare screes hang over verdant gorges; sullen tarns leach into bubbling mountain streams. The rivers in spate surge to lochs whipped white by the winds. Water is an elementary factor in my appreciation of this inimitable land. And that says a lot when Lochaber squelches in up to 12 ft of rain a year. Yet the abundance gives the hills perspective as well as their varied greens, tans and russets.

Once I would apologise to hitch-hikers and tourists met by chance for the torrent that doused their stay in the glen. Then I ditched excuses, for visitors rarely protest about Argyll's weather (the sabre-toothed midge is something else), certainly if they are not tenting and hail from abroad. West Highland scenery performs regardless of the deluge and tourists invariably applaud. Weather blues are a local refrain, but then the indigenous people endure the stair-rods of an annual autumn monsoon, sometimes for months on end.

When the rains came I would sometimes trace the source of a burn, a rewarding project on dreich days when climbing or guiding on the hill was out of the question. The quiet profusion of hue in secret niches, especially in spring and autumn, drew me back repeatedly. Once I fell in the River Coe trying to reach a precarious wild geranium my wife had located. It was worth the dooking for the purplish bloom brighten our small rockery from June to August.

The 1,500 ft climb of Clachaig Gully is famed in spring for its secluded riot of pale-yellow primroses. Moss campion displays scarce rose-pink petals on rocky shelves of brooks and I've also decked the rockery with a yellow saxifrage cutting from a dripping corner of the Buachaille waterslide. Even common cotton grass waves alluringly around an oily peat tarn and hairbells quiver in surprise against grey walls. Radiant colour will blaze from every other dreary corner, if the

From a rocky seat under Great Gully on Buachaille Etive Mor, the view sweeps to the Devil's Staircase at Altnafeadh, and the Mamores.

Overleaf: Autumn gold and green on the banks of the River Coe at Carnoch.

eye is not oblivious. And fauna is abundant as flora, though there is camouflage here too. The faded rump of a red deer even at a distance is an instant eye-opener to a stalker but a small herd vanishes before the casual observer on the hill.

Buzzards are far more ordinary than many folk imagine and are regularly mistaken for golden eagles. They hardly compare in size at maturity for the eagle's wingspan is around half the spread again of its cousin. A buzzard's breast and tail seen from below are lightly flecked while the eagle is darker with paler markings confined more to the wings. The call of the eagle is a distinct, kyaa and at times a whistle.

Once, on the summit of Gear Aonach, the mid-sibling of the Three Sisters, on a grey winter's morn I came across a set of blue hare tracks in the snow. They swung towards the edge of a small cornice, smoothly at first, then doubled back to a few dramatic droplets of blood. Curious at the stark stain on virgin snow I moved closer and the fate of the hare became apparent. Imprinted in the plush surface were the spear-shaped primary feathers of a golden eagle. The beauty of the mountains is marred at times by tragedy.

Eagles themselves are threatened sometimes by the unscrupulous and though I suspect the sites of half-a-dozen nesting pairs I have never sought or cared to know the precise location of an eyrie. *Aquila chrysaetos* wisely wheels clear of *Homo sapiens*, and vice versa.

Most laws have an exception and I experienced an encounter of these species that I welcomed, even envied. Sitting above the Meeting of Three Waters opposite the Lost Valley, or Coire Gabhail, I watched a green hang-glider floating at around 4,000 ft above the short ridge of Gearr Aonach. The sky was clear and in the warm sun I felt compelled to stay for half an hour. In the lightest breeze, the flier swung abruptly from his arc and crossed to Aonach Dubh in a long shallow dive. His quest was a golden eagle turning in the middle of the glen, a gilded carnivore no longer the master of all he surveyed.

Together, man and bird spiralled on the thermal in cautious,

Broad Gully and the stark cliffs of Stob Coire nan Lochan .

Craig Caldwell camped beneath
the Zig-Zags of Gearr Aonach.
The entry below to Lost Valley
leads to the peaks of Stob Coire nan
Lochan (distant) and Bidean nam
Bian.

Rowland and Mark Edwards
savour the quality of Satan's Slit,
Buachaille Etive Mor.

The serrated ridge of Aonach Eagach (top).

Lost Valley and Stob Coire nan Lochan from the Gorge. (above)

Reedy Loch Achtriochtan and Aonach Eagach (right).

mutual respect. Another pair of eagles approached from near Meall Mor and the glider pilot widened his circle to draw them in. Gradually all four joined the stack under Aonach Dubh's air traffic control, elemental aviators flying in harmony – and strange beauty in the eye of the beholder.

Wildcats are scarce by my experience in Glen Coe and keep a low profile. Two and three times the size of a domestic feline they escape by a whisker on the night prowl from fast cars in the heart of the glen. We have seen them at the bracken edge under a rocky outcrop just beyond some sycamores at Achtriochtan.

The fox is equally shy but proliferates, as intelligence deserves and the purges of recent years by local sheep farmers adequately confirm. I confronted a big dog once on the first of the Three Sisters, Beinn Fhada, the long ridge. Bushed out in his full winter glory, reynard turned flaming tail and bounding ahead through the snow cut sharply down a steep gully. There was no risk of me trying to follow in that defile

It may surprise, but the creature of cunning in the lowland woodlands and around the city limits has a talented climbing cousin venturing widely in the mountains. Dog and vixen stalk ptarmigan, mice and other varied fare from the lower glen to the highest summits in all seasons. Keeping an alert yellow eye open, of course, for the most deadly of all predators – Man.

Red deer easily outnumber sheep in the wider Glencoe mountains and are more widespread through the range. They blend superbly with the landscape and especially in autumn among the deer grass sprouting golden brown on the slopes. Startled, an older hind will cough an alert to others feeding nearby and the shapely ladies, five to fifteen animals, go loping uphill with remarkable speed and elegance. A few may halt briefly to inspect the intruder or test the air from a distant ridge, then turn out of sight. Stags forage apart from hinds and the younger deer until rut or mating begins in summer.

Deer spend the days usually in remote corries and on quiet

Approach through the deer grass to the summer climbs of the Buachaille, near Bridge of Etive.

hillsides away from traffic flows, human and vehicular, though half-a-dozen stags often graze brazenly on more luxuriant grass at Huan Findlay's farm, Achtriochtan, on the busy A82. The antlered beasts vanish when the half-dozen local estate owners, including the Forestry Commission and the National Trust for Scotland begin calling; in September to November for stag-culling and by February for hinds. In the autumn rut, the echo of roaring stags can be heard even in the more popular walking glens such as Coire Gabhail, the coire of capture, where the reiving Macdonalds are reputed to have secreted stolen cattle.

A consequence of the gradual destruction of the great Caledonian woods is that the red deer of today is a mere shadow of the animal known to our ancestors. In the natural forest the animals had protection not only from predators but from the enervating Scottish winters. Their decline in size and weight is directly attributable to the lack of that habitual cover and rich feeding the woods provide, much as they do now for the smaller roe deer around villages and towns. A Highland stag would once stand around six feet at the shoulder instead of the more usual four today and weigh gralloched, or gutted, some thirty stones or more than half the weight again of any recent monarch of the glen.

In a vicious winter the red deer fight a war of attrition, dying widely from cold and malnutrition. Scouring the mountain fastness for the grass, moss, heather and tree shoots they need to survive is a relentless affair that often brings herds down to the roadsides and human habitations for easier foraging. They manage remarkably well on the whole for the Red Deer Commission now urges Scottish landowners to improve their cullings to reduce the estimated national herd of some 300,000 red deer to a more manageable and humane 240,000.

Highland airs waft in the hills at the Glencoe and Loch Leven Music Festival . . . Iona MacColl and Allan Scott (left) and local hoteliers Nairn McArthur, Morag Mackintosh and James MacLeod (above). The swing of the kilts at Ballachulish Gala Day (right).

CHAPTER SEVEN

A Clan Skirmish

The old Telford road above The
Study (left) was extended to
Glencoe from the Devil's Staircase.
View south from the An t-Sron
ridge (above).

THE SUSTAINED GRANDEUR of Glen Coe is a magnet not only for climbers and mountaineers. By far the greatest invasion of the glen is by tourists and hillwalkers of every nationality. They come in the early mode of writers and poets inspired by the Waverley novels of Sir Walter Scott, to breathe the beauty and maybe the romance of Scotland. Most visitors arrive via Loch Lomondside and from Oban or Bridge of Orchy. Walkers trek the 95-mile West Highland Way and depart over the Devil's Staircase to Kinlochleven. Some walk in the green lairigs of Gartain and Eilde, up into the sanctuary of the Lost Valley or on the crests of Aonach Eagach and Bidean nam Bian. In such moody terrain, a sound hill apprenticeship is wise.

Drizzle and mist shift in fast, even in summer – or more so. Navigation on the heights can be a problem in any season, like hypothermia. Ann and I once crashed a students' Highland ceilidh on a lofty glen arete during a brief snowstorm – in mid-June! Dancing, in shorts and T-shirts, was essential just to keep warm. Lack of mountain acumen causes injury or worse. Weatherdial, the forecast phone check is reliable and the Scottish Avalanche Project gives accurate risk alerts on strategic noticeboards in the glen.

A light snow flurry at the close of a January day's skiing a few years ago sprang to a blizzard and hurricane-force winds so rapidly that coaches from the slopes and numerous cars and lorries were trapped on the A82 between White Corries and Black Mount. Only the determined efforts of police and rescuers got a convoy of makeshift four-wheel drive vehicles with more than 100 skiers, including children, safely over the watershed near Lagangarbh and down to the lower glen. Most had elected to stay aboard their coaches overnight, heated by the diesel engines and watching video films to pass the hours. They changed their minds quickly when the buses lifted violently in the 100 mph gusts.

Glencoe Mountain Rescue Team was founded in 1962 by the tall, bearded Hamish MacInnes a few years after he came to the glen to

Blizzards frequently sweep upper Glen Coe and catch out drivers, though gritting and ploughing on the A82 has improved immensely. Wildlife and estate animals (left) are deprived of grazing.

Digging out vehicles after a night's snowfall is routine at Altnafeadh, the burn of the bogs, at close to 800 ft.

Overleaf:
Lagangarbh, the rough hollow, and the Scottish Mountaineering Club hut at the head of Lairig Gartain – below the Coire na Tulaich track to the summit of Buachaille Etive Mor.

In pain from a pelvic injury, Robert Campbell miraculously survived a 1,000 ft fall down Buachaille Etive Mor. His slide, over a series of walls, began in the snows beneath the stretcher (right) and ended where rescuers stand.

live, climb and develop mountain gear. Before this era, rescues were largely the prerogative of the Elliot family who have long occupied the small white cottage on Loch Achtriochtan, under Aonach Dubh. Usually with the local bobby, a shepherd or casual hill-goer Elliot senior and sons would climb the hill and collect the casualty. Walter, a sheep farmer, and Willie, the local National Trust for Scotland ranger, are still staunch members of the 20-man team.

With only 1,500 people in the Glencoe catchment area the funding of a voluntary civilian team, notably when a pair of plastic boots now cost upward of £150, is problematic at any time. Northern Constabulary and the Scottish Office defray much expense but finance is a perpetual concern. Police act in liaison with the team and call-outs are co-ordinated from a well-equipped radio truck parked off-duty at Hamish's home and workshop at the foot of the glen. Climbers make best team-members, obviously, because of the Glen Coe terrain and the

Another casualty, on Aonach Dubh, is off by air to the Belford Hospital, Fort William. Will Thomson hopes for a lull.

need for activists who know every cliff and summit intimately. But men bred to the hills, like Peter Weir, a forestry worker who has devised with his wife Rosemary one of the most comfortable and popular B&Bs in Lochaber, is vital for his natural strength and skills. Competent on the hill but a non-climber, Peter will remark as the twin-jet RAF Wessex or Sea King helicopter revs for take off, 'I hope I remembered to pack the toilet paper.'

Glencoe rescuers often seem a random job-lot but there is a fair self-reliance and resourcefulness in the structure. More than half the team are self-employed in fishing, forestry, computer science, engineering, mountain guiding and gear and avalanche research.

As yet, every member is male, maybe largely because of the scarcity of rugged local women climbers who fancy lugging 15-stone casualties a couple of mountain miles on a stretcher from the outback, or down 3,000 ft of wet snow, scree and broken track when the choppers are grounded by cloud or high winds. Rescue takes character – back uphill, maybe, twice at night after a climbing day – and characters. John

Flt. Lt. Al Coy, former commander B Flight, 22 Squadron, RAF Leuchars. A climber and fine mountain rescue flier.

An alpine ambiance (far left) on the easy trek from Stob Coire Leith to Sgor nam Fiannaidh. No descent is advised before the end of the ridge.

A magnificent Scottish hillwalk and scramble – the Aonach Eagach. Derek Lloyd negotiates the pinnacles above sheer drops to the River Coe and Loch Leven.

Walkers pause at the steep descent from Am Bodach at the start of the east to west traverse of the ridge (left).

Grieve, for example, a qualified teacher, rock and ice climber and ex-instructor, former solo scallop diver now supplies the Continent commercially with quality smoked seafoods and pâté that food writers should have been on to long ago. Much like Hamish, John is the dedicated rescue type, an aspect of which might be that he also knows the trauma of being rescued himself. Grieve survived but lost three friends in an avalanche accident on Ben Nevis.

Hamish is a man with a remarkable hatrack. Climber, writer, cameraman, expert rescuer, climbing and rescue-equipment designer and technical butler to the gentry of feature and TV film-making with a mountain connection. Film companies are enamoured of the glen's attributes as much for TV commercial backdrop as for stunning effect on the big screen. As in *Highlander*, the fantasy set in Scotland's past and New York's present.

Many locals, including John Grieve and craftshop owner Dave Cooper, prospered from the production, as film extras or suppliers. A clan skirmish betwen those in tartan of a blue hue and those in green, a coincidental choice so close to sectarian Glasgow, attracted many summer tourists. A rout was arranged aptly under Buachaille Etive Beg and close to Lochan na Fola, the bloody waters. Director Russell Mulcahy raised his megaphone and made it clear, at least to an avid and hushed public, that with the call, 'Death to the Macleods', the greens were to rush downhill and clash with the blues, and nothing more.

This was nearly accomplished, to the obvious approval of the onlookers and Mr Mulcahy who knows star quality when he sees it. The trouble was that the megaphone failed to get the call 'cut', across the din of pipes and the clang of swords and targes, to the highlanders. Straight from a liquid King's House lunch, many fought with spirit, some seemingly settling old and grievous scores. A few fell in the bog and were used as bridges by others anxious to keep their feet dry. One gallant needed three stitches in a face wound, raising his minimum £20 a day and bonus of £30 by another £100 a stitch, it was stated. An older

John Grieve, climber, diver, rescuer – sea-food specialist!

clansman not in the best of trim for these exertions was stretchered from the field.

Frenchman Christopher Lambert was the leading man and Sean Connery an excellent runner-up. By tradition, the stars buy crew and cast a drink at the final rap. James Bond, apparently, was shaken more than stirred at his King's House dram bill said to be a sum not far detached from £1,000. *Highlander* went down like a lead balloon when shown in Lochaber a year or so later, but folk here take the scenery for granted. Apparently it grossed enough for the making of *Highlander 2*, which is imminent, I believe.

Some stalwarts of the local rescue team should not be allowed to pass, though now retired from similar exertion. Huan Findlay and his

A spirited attack on the MacLeods under Buachaille Etive Beg – a dramatic episode in the feature film 'Highlander'.

Christopher Lambert, star of 'Highlander'. (far left)

Sometimes, though, it is the sheep farmers who need a hand and rescuers go out to save the ewes. Not long ago a local shepherd Alistair MacDonald of Carnoch found the recovery of two of his prized blackface animals from the opposite walls of a dank, 250 ft chasm in Glen Etive a bit of a handful for one man. Dave Cooper and I went back with him, humphing ropes and other technical devices. It did not take long to get Alistair's drift. The first ewe was on a sloping rock ledge festooned with black ice and the drop was mesmerising. Dave tied in to the ropes below a tree and boulder belay. Skidding on ice while grappling with the sheep which seemed determined to throw the both of us down the dunny, was about as much climbing excitement as I care to devise. Lassoing the second dam, shoving her up a sub-tropical jungle while occasionally the ledge below collapsed sending me pedalling in space on the rope was an even more theatrical farce. But we stomped off the hill in the dark well, pleased with the day's work and looking forward to a dram.

Huan Findlay, who lives in the heart of the glen under Aonach Eagach and the great scree fall that has newly been designated a Sight of Special Scientific Interest (perhaps to inhibit folk hauling the landscape away) has 1,100 blackface and 13 Highland cattle.

As a tenant of the NTS, the be-whiskered Huan was encouraged to acquire the woolly herd partly as a tourist attraction, he says. Though they take a wheen of winter feeding and make little profit the visitors addicted to tartanalia and all things Scotch dig them very much. Alistair wife Kathleen have lived at Achtriochtan farm for 25 years and a charming couple they are. Over six feet tall and a rugby devotee Huan often enjoyed the sensible revelry conducted by Rory Macdonald, proprietor then of the Clachaig Inn, in the snug bar. Life in the glen as a sheep farmer is a trying enough labour of love without the added stress, physical and sometimes intellectual, of evacuating casualties. Huan did both in the bad old days before aircraft, playing in the most testing position, between the shafts of a MacInnes stretcher, on long carries down abominable hills often in the dark, sleet and wind.

Highland cattle and sheep need much supplementary feed to survive relentless rain, frost and blizzard. Mountain farmer Ronnie McLauchlan (far right) used helicopters to reach his starving Blackface ewes.

Previous page: Glencoe and Ballachulish are havens for yachts people making passage to the Western Isles. The former slate village of Ballachulish is being restored as an admirable tourist centre.

MacDonald has some 700 sheep in all, not in the old Glencoe common grazing at Kingshouse which has lost popularity so near the A82, but again on tenanted NTS land in Glen Etive. Walter Elliot farms ewes for an Italian landowner managing his own cattle affairs in the Great Glen. Willie has some sheep of his own and another 500 or so belong to an absentee Belgian count at Black Corries Estate. Traffic takes a high toll of sheep in the largely unfenced glen, up to 60 a year and many lambs at Achtriochtan.

July is an arduous month with the gather of the sheep from all airts of the glen, the clipping, dipping and then the worry about prices to be fetched at Dalmally, Stirling or Corpach. Income would not induce many to take up shepherding. 'You could make more some years leaving the money in the bank,' Huan asserts.

Kathleen and her husband have reared a tall son and daughter in the small, wood-panelled cottage nestling between the bulwarks of Aonach Dubh and Aonach Eagach. Alan is studying agriculture in Aberdeen and may follow his father's calling (or whistling) with sheep in the glen. As the recently retired head teacher at Glencoe Primary School, Kathleen has a few daft tales about local children. I like a lot the story of a Black Corries lad years ago who asked his dad one day if he could include gran in his diverse bird and animal skull collection when she passed on.

There is less to be amused at in Glencoe these days. Open access and the very fabric of Scotland's vaunted mountain areas are more under threat than ever. Those intent on retaining the essential outdoor freedom of movement where easy access and restricted development have been traditional, voice concern, rightly in my opinion. Prime examples are proposals for major tourist projects at Clachaig Inn and the erection now of three miles of ugly barbed-wire fencing opposite Buachaille Etive Mor. Agricultural exemption from planning restraints in such areas must be questioned. Mineral extraction from rivers and gullies need closer monitoring. For many years, W H Murray, a stylish writer, mountaineer and a pillar of the NTS fought to preserve the glen, to eliminate posts, waymarkers and other eyesores. The task would seem to require renewal.

Huan Findlay with crummock and the miner's lamp that threw light on many a dark Glencoe rescue.

Glencoe is a buttress of the national heritage. Its defence, and that includes an overview of adjacent properties, must be the dominant principle of its management. Though the National Trust for Scotland has sought always to act as a responsible custodian, and the public has much to be grateful for, its stewardship is now in question. Pressures today on the NTS bear no relation to the climate in the 1930s. Increasing responsibilities, with more than 100 superlative properties, stretch its resources and, it would seem, its capabilities. Percy Unna, a former president of the Scottish Mountaineering Club disbursed a personal fortune in helping the NTS to acquire much of Glencoe in 1935 from

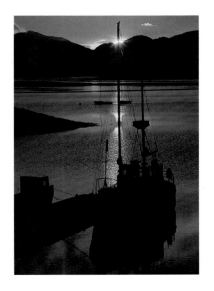

Lord Strathcona (as well as Kintail which he paid for outright and anonymously as usual).

In 1937, the SMC co-opted the British Mountaineering Council to help secure Dalness when it came on the market, and again the Danish-born engineer made generous provision. Before his death in 1950 Unna also made bequests to the NTS to help maintain their mountain properties, an act of generosity in fact to every hillgoer who esteems Glencoe.

Percy Unna loved the mountains dearly and sought to keep artifacts such as Glencoe exactly as they were. He did not approve of civilisation's amenity and clutter and would certainly have disapproved of the bridges that now give safe and easy access to the Lost Valley and Stob Coire nan Lochan. Whether to dismantle them now and protect these sanctuaries from the rising people pressure of today, risking lives in the raging River Coe and adding considerably to the task of rescue evacuation, remains a contentious issue.

Unna's famed 10 stipulations are perhaps flawed, here and there, in today's analysis. But a sub-section of one pertinent paragraph in the questions of management he put to the NTS in 1937 says at its close, 'It is hoped that the Trust may be able to come to an understanding with neighbouring proprietors as to corresponding restriction being maintained in regard to land near to that held by the Trust.' And that, I sense, is the nub.

Autumn larch, looking east on Loch Leven to the Pap of Glencoe and Kinlochleven.

A peaceful mooring at Bishop's Bay with views to the great horseshoe of Beinn a' Bheithir (left). Liquid gold Linnhe, and Ballachulish pier (above left).

While the NTS of late faces controversy and may now be re-considering a latent plan to extend the sprawling tourist centre at Clachaig, it is more the potential threat to a designated area of outstanding beauty from adjacent commercial interests that requires to be addressed. Glencoe is a priceless yet fragile mountain sanctuary esteemed worldwide. It is there to be loved and appreciated not simply by a generation, but by all people for all time. It's protection concerns all of us, individually and collectively, and is something we can never afford to take for granted.

Bibliography

Scotland's Mountains, W H Murray (Scottish Mountaineering Club, 1987)

Central Highlands, P Hodgkiss (Scottish Mountaineering Club, 1984)

Scottish Climbs 1, Hamish MacInnes (Constable, 1981)

Sweep Search, Hamish MacInnes (Hodder, 1985)

Rock and Ice Climbs, Glencoe and Glenetive, Ken Crocket (Scottish Mountaineering Club, 1980)

Scrambles in Lochaber, Noel Williams (Cicerone, 1985)

A Guide to the West Highland Way, Tom Hunter (Constable, 1979)

Glencoe: The Story of the Massacre, John Prebble (Penguin, 1969)

The Drove Roads of Scotland, A R B Haldane (Edinburgh University Press, 1968)

Glencoe (The National Trust for Scotland, 1986)

Hamish's Mountain Walk, Hamish Brown (Paladin, 1980)

Mountaineering in Scotland, W H Murray (Diadem, 1979)

West Highland Walks 1, Hamish MacInnes (Hodder, 1984)

The Western Highlands, Tom Weir (Batsford, 1973)

Monarchs of the Glen, Duff Hart-Davis (Jonathan Cape, 1978)